DEAR
INNER
CRITIC

Also by Rebecca Kuder

The Eight Mile Suspended Carnival

DEAR INNER CRITIC

A self-doubt
activity book

Rebecca Kuder

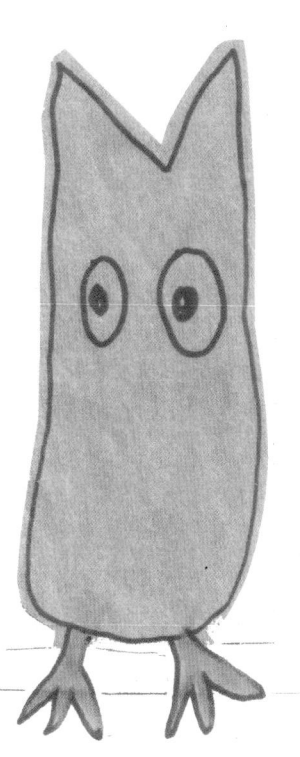

REBECCA KUDER

Copyright © 2024 Rebecca Kuder.

All rights reserved. No part of this book may be reproduced or transmitted in any form or by any means without written permission from the author.

ISBN: 978-1-950272-22-8

Cover art, untitled (Dear Inner Critic), paper collage on spiral notebook, copyright © 2024 Rebecca Kuder.

Author self-portrait inspired by GravityWorks Circus, copyright © 2024 Rebecca Kuder.

Book design by Alligator Tree Graphics, alligatortreegraphics.com.

Excerpt from "The Ballad of Solomon Jones" by Jon Langford. Copyright © 2011, Low Noise Music (ASCAP). Used by permission. All rights reserved.

Printed by Mixam.

First edition 1 2 3 4 5 6 7 8 9

Literary Kitchen
www.literarykitchen.net

To Hummy and MSKW, with infinite love.
To all who find relief inside this book.
And to my own dear inner critic,
who has never achieved a permanent name.

CONTENTS

START HERE	3
How To Use This Book	3
What Is The Inner Critic?	4
Before You Explore	9

DISCOVERY

1. ASSEMBLE YOUR GREETERS	21
2. POWER POSE	23
3. DRAW A SELF-PORTRAIT	25
4. DANCE PARTY	26
5. DRAW THE INNER CRITIC	28
6. DEAR INNER CRITIC (A LETTER)	30
7. WRITE A DIALOGUE	32
8. MAKE A SCENE	33
9. DRAW A COMIC	35
10. NOTICE AND COUNTERACT	37

BOUNDARIES AND BUSY WORK

11. NONVIOLENCE? REALLY?	41
12. GET A JOB	43
13. PERFECT COMEBACKS	45
14. DESIGNATE SPACE	47
15. TO DO TODAY	49

16. FUTURE FRIEND	51
17. VERY CONTRARY	52
18. IMAGINE A CHEERLEADER	53
19. PERFORMANCE REVIEW	55
20. AN UNEXPECTED GIFT	56

TOWARD (SELF-)COMPASSION

21. SOUNDS OF DISTRESS	59
22. WHO CARES WHAT THEY NEED?	60
23. HOW YOU PROVED (OR WILL PROVE) THEM WRONG	61
24. CHOOSE YOUR OWN ADVENTURE	62
25. DEAR RISK MANAGER	64
26. WHAT ARE THEY TRYING TO TELL YOU?	66
27. A DIFFERENT GIFT	68
28. THE SANDBOX	69
29. DEAR YOU	70
30. EMPTY NEST	72
WHAT COMES NEXT?	73
More Activities	74
BACKSTORY AND ACKNOWLEDGEMENTS	78
RESOURCES	84
Understanding and Healing Trauma and Other Helpful Items	84
Writers, Music, and Other Sources of Inspiration	85
Self-Care and Nourishment	86
Literary Kitchen Publications	86

Sometimes you get what you ask for—
time to start asking for more.

—Jon Langford, "The Ballad of Solomon Jones"

START HERE

HOW TO USE THIS BOOK

The activities in this book will help you disarm, calm, and quiet the inner critic. Your relationship to self-doubt will evolve. My hope for you is that you find more room in your life for unfettered creativity and joy.

Use this book however you want—it's yours! You can do the activities on your own, or with a friend, or even a group of people.

Please allow yourself to be *curious*. My dictionary defines the word curious as 'desirous of learning or knowing; inquisitive.' The activities in this book are intentionally playful. When we approach what we do as a type of play, the stakes usually don't feel as high as when we aim to be productive. (Also, human beings learn through play, sometimes without even noticing.) Think in terms of experimentation. Process. *Let's see what happens.*

For maximum potency, do one activity each day for 30 days. Activities appear in an order that moves toward expanded creative freedom. But you can dive in however it works for you. Repeat or adapt any activity—I hope you will discover something new.

Before you start, I invite you to write down how you feel about self-doubt and your intention/s for this 30-day experiment. What are your expectations (if any)? What do you hope to learn, shift, or change about how self-doubt shows up in your life?

May anyone (and everyone) who reads these words find something useful here, toward self-love and liberation.

May future generations feel stronger in themselves through our work here, now.

WHAT IS THE INNER CRITIC?

If you are reading this book, it's likely you already grasp the concept of the inner critic, but let's take a moment to ponder the slippery entity that inhabits our thoughts and too often gives voice to self-doubt.

Consciously and unconsciously, self-doubt gets introduced into our creative beings from myriad sources. From large societal systems, and from other people who haven't learned another way. We mirror what we see in the world.

Patriarchy, systemic racism, capitalism—and all schemes

based on fear, control, manipulation, or oppression—do not encourage us to feel good about who we are.

Our experience of self-doubt is often shaped by who we are in relation to systems of power and privilege. Self-doubt spans all genders and identities and manifests in many ways. Often, self-doubt becomes an invisible, involuntary reflex. To liberate the creative heart takes time, attention, and work.

Self-doubt can be particularly brutal for women and other marginalized people. As a cisgender woman living in a patriarchal society, I have carried self-doubt as if there is no other way to be. I was not taught how to release myself from this burden. I was not taught to renegotiate my relationship to the inner critic.

Many of us experience self-doubt as an inner voice. You know it when you hear it. That voice creeps in and lurks, and says things like, "You're not good enough," or, "Who do you think you are?" Sometimes the voice repeats unhelpful messages received in the past—maybe from someone who held more power. If they take root, those messages can sound like truth, like fact.

Here's the good part: with practice, we can learn to release those messages. We can release them! Let that sink in.

Because self-doubt is so deeply ingrained, the inner critic's voice can sound like our own. It can take time to separate that voice from oneself. Maybe the voice was planted by the cultural assumption of not being good enough, or by someone specific in our past, or a teacher's red pen, or whatever wore us down, compressed or broke our spirit. Maybe it was whispered by the airbrushed perfection of *Seventeen Magazine*. Maybe it's fed and kept alive when we compare ourselves to the curated and digitally enhanced images that others share on social media. Whatever its origin/s, too many of us are dogged by that voice. With little or no warning, *my* inner critic can destabilize everything, including the writing process—it can stop me before I start.

That voice erodes joy.

What to do?

✷ ✷ ✷

In the 1990s, I took a feminist self-defense class in Seattle called Alternatives to Fear. One theme was how to maximize resources—how to gather and use information about a situation and place. Let's say I'm walking alone at night in an isolated area. I hear footsteps behind me. My nervous system triggers the fight, flight, or freeze response. This physiological response is all about survival. It's a biological reflex, to protect me when I am under threat. *There's someone following me.* (I feel scared.) *Do I ignore the sound? Walk faster? Run?*

Or do I turn around and see who's there?

If I remain in that fight, flight, or freeze response, my nervous system stays activated. It's hard to think. But if I can re-engage my thinking brain, I can remind myself that I have options. If I turn around, I gain information, a resource that helps me assess the situation and determine whether there's an actual threat. And with this resource, it's easier to keep myself safe, if needed, or to calm my nervous system if there's no real danger.

To engage with the inner critic can be similar: who's there? Who's behind that voice? Who's doubted me for so long I can't recall when it started? Why are they following me? What is the real (or perceived) threat? What do they want or need?

An important digression about the nervous system: When we are threatened—when we experience a shock trauma, when something happens that feels like *too much, too soon,* or *too fast*—our bodies react to keep us safe. *Fight, flight, or freeze.* However, if we don't release that activation of the nervous system, we can unintentionally store the trauma in our bodies, so at other times, we react in that fight, flight, or freeze pattern, even when we are not in danger. We keep running when no one is chasing us. Learning to regulate the nervous system is possible and powerful. One simple breathing technique that can help is 4-7-8 breathing: inhale for four counts, hold your breath for seven counts, and exhale for eight counts. (See **Resources** at the end of this book.) For more information about how all this works and what to do about it, see *The Body Keeps The Score* by Bessel van der Kolk.

Sometimes the inner critic is a self-appointed risk manager. Not a simple villain! Maybe that inner voice is assessing danger. Trying to keep us safe from a real (or perceived) threat.

I have come to know my inner critic as a wounded and scared part of myself, so I practice compassion. This awareness came to me after lots of time telling off (i.e., cursing at) the inner critic. Expressing my rage was crucial. After I had done that for a while, I got calmer. Then I got curious. Eventually, I was able to converse with my inner critic. To work toward balance.

As you use this activity book, you'll figure out what you need, and what your relationship to the inner critic needs. This practice can transform how the dynamic works. I know my inner critic really well now, and we have developed a clumsy kind of rapport. I feel a lot better. Making room for the relationship to evolve has been a real help in my writing and my life.

We are each made from many parts.[†] The inner critic

[†] Internal Family Systems—the notion that we all contain different parts of the self—informed some ideas in this book.

is a part of us, and all our parts are important. But too often the inner critic gets in the way of pleasure and peace.

Let's not continue to accept extraneous chatter and injury. Let's not shrink, hide, or run away. Running away has never worked for me. What if we stop running, turn around, see who's there, and engage in conversation? What if we use playful, creative tactics to revise the dance, set some boundaries, and write—into our bodies and spirits—a new narrative?

Let's get curious.

BEFORE YOU EXPLORE

Take Care of Yourself

Even if you've been living with self-doubt all your life, today can be different. You're still alive and you can try something new. The capacity to heal is real. The imagination is powerful.

While you access and explore self-doubt, I want to help you feel safe. I intend the framework in these pages to support a sense of well-being. I want you to know (and feel) that, in doing this work, you are not in danger. These activities can empower, exhilarate, and energize. They can also numb, challenge, or upset. Perusing the inner self can be complicated. Sometimes the messages received throughout life make us feel not good enough, and those beliefs can be hard to overthrow. Maybe the messages came from others who were taught *they* were not good enough, who never questioned that notion, and without ill will, passed their trauma along to us. We inherit things and we pass them on. Sometimes even the playful activities in this book can interact with ancient shame about who we are or who we are allowed to be. Negative messages and beliefs—*instilled how long ago? during which generation? who can remember?*—become background static that we cease to notice, but still *feel*.

Maybe—without conscious thought—we start to accept those negative messages as truth. When we unearth what is so deeply held, we may feel vulnerable. We may have messy emotions. It helps to anticipate that wobble, and plan how to take care of ourselves.

Everyone has wounds. How we understand and deal with our wounds can shape how the wounds persist or mend.

Vulnerability is natural, and expected, and it's okay. Please pay attention to what these activities bring up for you. Trust your gut. If you feel fragile, you can slow down . . . slow down even more . . . or step away. Come back another time. Self-care is important and noble. Simple ideas: drink water; go outside; close your eyes and breathe slowly for a few moments; listen to a song that makes you feel good. Sing along. Watch the sun set. Watch the sun rise. Talk to a trusted person, pet, tree, or stuffed animal. This 30-day experiment is an embodied practice, so please take care of your body (and what's inside, too).

If what comes up feels too overwhelming or unmanageable, please consider seeking professional support. Somatic Experiencing (a method of treating trauma-based conditions by modifying the nervous system's stress response) offers ways to handle the feelings and reactions that might come up as you experiment with these activities. For more information, please see **Resources** at the end of this book.

A note about generosity: Many people have been taught the value of being generous to others. We may not have learned how to be generous to ourselves. I hope this book will offer you the ability to imagine the possibility of being more generous with yourself. The possibility of being less miserly with self-care. The possibility of valuing and prioritizing your needs, too. To find a balance between taking care of self and others requires practice, but it's possible to achieve. It's absolutely possible, and vital, to be less stingy and more generous with yourself.

Gather Supplies

You'll need something to write on and with. Inspired by the work of Lynda Barry,[†] I like to use:

- Blank index cards (for drawing, notes, lists of bonus points, or helpful reminders and slogans, etc.);
- Pen (see below);
- A notebook or any paper (such as Roaring Spring composition books);
- Stopwatch or kitchen timer (ideally analog and not your phone);
- Optional: colored pens or pencils or crayons;
- Optional: those little foil star stickers from the office supply store (like the ones on the cover of this book).

Choose a pen with smooth ink flow. I love a refillable fountain pen or a black Flair. I don't love a ballpoint. Too scratchy. I want a pleasant tactile experience. Find what works for you. Don't overthink the quest. It's absolutely fine to use what you already have.

But I do recommend you use a pen. If you use a pencil—please, please resist the urge to erase. The urge to erase is

[†] Lynda Barry is a cartoonist/graphics artist, teacher, and MacArthur Genius.

often a reflexive response to unhelpful chatter from the inner critic. And even with a pen, resist the urge to cross things out. Just do your thing, live with it, and move on. Release perfectionism! It's okay. We're all human, and that's beautiful.

Avoid using your phone or computer while doing the activities. If you need to use a device for accessibility, please turn off that nagging, judgmental spelling and grammar check, where the inner critic is known to hide.

Give yourself foil stars whenever you want or need them. When I'm teaching, I bring sheets of stars to class and scatter them on the tables so people can reward themselves as needed.

How To Prepare For An Activity

Before you start an activity, gather supplies. Refer back to the opening pages of this book. Settle into your body. I like the one-minute spiral from Lynda Barry: start with a small dot, then very slowly (even slower than you can imagine) draw a spiral outward from the dot. You can find videos online to see her spiral in action. Make the spiral as tight as you can without letting the lines touch. Slow, slow, slower. Even slower. Just spiral and breathe for a long moment. Then prepare to explore.

Guidelines For Timed Freewriting[†]

1. Tell your inner critic to leave the room.
2. You don't have to read or share what you write, unless you want to.
3. Take a deep breath. Let your body relax.
4. Set the timer. Put your pen on the paper.
5. Start writing.
6. Keep writing. Keep breathing.
7. No need to worry about spelling, punctuation, or grammar.
8. Follow the thoughts and words. No need to *stay on topic*. No need to *make sense*.
9. If you run out of words, write *tick tick tick* until other words come out.
10. Keep the pen moving across the paper. Resist any urge to erase or cross out.
11. When the time is up, stop.
12. Exhale, stretch, shake, etc., as your body needs.

[†] Adapted from Natalie Goldberg and Lynda Barry.

Drawing is fun!

Or at least it used to be fun. And it can be fun again.

For these drawing activities, there's only one rule: No stick figures.

Why? Because we have bodies. No one I know is a stick figure.

Maybe you already know how to draw a person who is not made of sticks. If so, okay! Make a frame and draw your person.

If you believe you can only draw stick figures, prepare to have your mind blown and prove your inner critic wrong. You don't even need to *be creative* or *be an artist,* whatever that means.

Try it now—here's how!

Guidelines For Drawing[†]

1. On an index card, notebook page, or any paper, draw a rectangle (a frame to contain the image).
2. In the frame, draw a shape for a head.
3. Draw a shape for a body (attached to the head).
4. Draw two parallel-ish lines for each limb. The lines do not need to be straight.
5. Draw each hand and foot.
6. Draw a face (eyes, nose, mouth, ears, and don't forget eyebrows).
7. Draw hair, clothing, distinguishing features, props, etc.
8. Decorate the background, etc.
9. Sit back and admire your non-stick figure. Say hello!

[†] Adapted from Ivan Brunetti and Lynda Barry.

I drew this person in about three minutes. I cheated by not drawing the top of the head, which I left open for hair, then followed the steps to make the body, limbs, etc. and her legs became a tree trunk.

For a timed drawing (like a timed freewrite), keep your hand moving. If you think you're finished before time's up, keep going. Add textures, patterns, color it in, whatever. Keep drawing until the time is up.

Extra credit:
Do you ever notice yourself thinking things like *I'm not creative*, or *I can't draw,* or *I'm not an artist?* If so—stop right

there. Exchange that chatter for a feel-good message. Here are some ideas: *I am made of stardust, like we all are. I am allowed to draw and write and do fun things even if I haven't done them for a long time, even if I don't have experience, and even if someone said I couldn't! Or shouldn't!*

DISCOVERY I

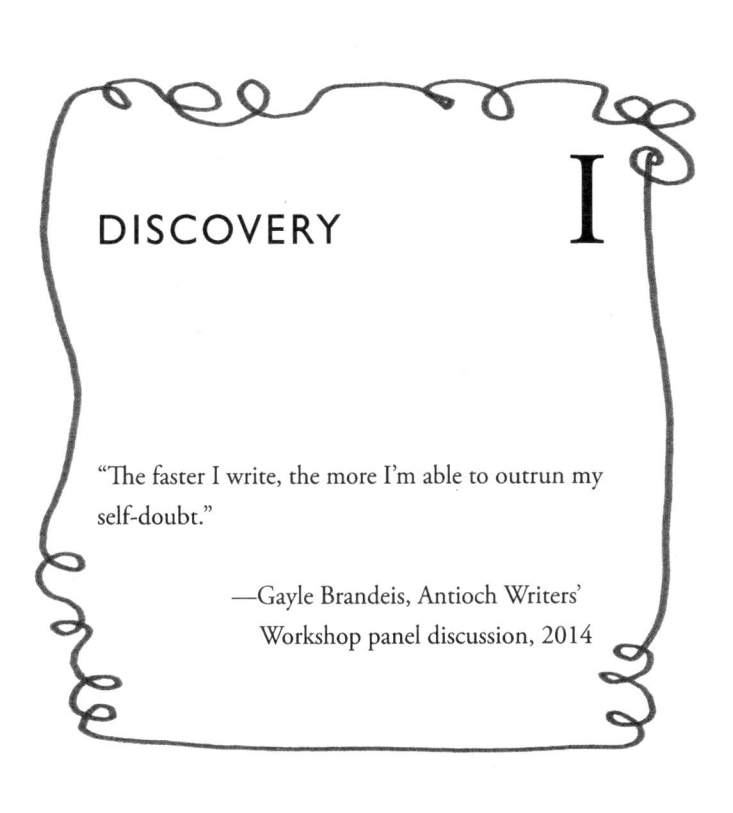

"The faster I write, the more I'm able to outrun my self-doubt."

—Gayle Brandeis, Antioch Writers' Workshop panel discussion, 2014

ASSEMBLE YOUR GREETERS

1

Refer to previous section **Take Care of Yourself**.

If you feel nervous about exploring stuff that might be difficult or painful, know this: It is possible to delve for a short, predetermined amount of time, then return to the safety of the present moment. Air and light will be waiting for you. Plan your ascent before you go down.

Gather your greeters. Make a list of helpful beings. Who will be there to embrace or help? Who will guide you back toward light? Greeters might be dead or alive, personally known to you or not. You might include people, places, or things that have inspired, helped, or sustained you in the past. Greeters might be delectable food or activities. A song. You can animate inanimate objects! Maybe it's a cozy sweater or blanket or stuffed animal—who says your teddy bear can't help you emerge from underground? Maybe it's a blue clay bowl someone made for you, or some other

---

This chapter was adapted from the work of Laraine Herring and Amy Rebekah Chavez.

artwork. This is your imagination, after all. Choose greeters who let you feel beloved and safe. Make a list of your greeters.

ALSO: List anything or anyone who is BANNED from greeting you (the non-greeters).

Keep this list handy. Add foil stars if you want to.

Extra credit:

Five minute freewrite: what do you notice about your list? Start with the phrase *I notice,* and come back to that phrase whenever you need to.

POWER POSE

2

Maybe you've seen Amy Cuddy's TED talk about power poses. The claim is about body language. If you take a power pose for even two minutes, this action rewires your brain to feel more confident. Examples: stand like Wonder Woman, feet apart, hands on hips; or sit with hands behind head and lean back in a chair and maybe put feet on a desk. Although the original study could not be replicated, the practice works for me.

Even if it's a placebo effect, why not try it?

Choose a power pose that is comfortable and doable. You can sit or stand. You might reach your arms out or up, or put your hands on hips, shoulders down . . . whatever works for you body. Only do what's comfortable. Hold the pose and remember to *breathe*. If something feels uncomfortable, change to another pose that feels better. Breathe. *See* your body expanding. *See* your body not shrinking.

Give yourself permission to take up space. Breathe.

Take up space in this way for two minutes or longer.

Do this practice every day, or any day, or today. Try other poses. Enjoy the quest for a pose that feels good.

Extra credit:
Using the guidelines for drawing on page 16, draw a picture of yourself doing a power pose.

DRAW A SELF-PORTRAIT 3

Review the guidelines for drawing.

Start with a frame.

Set a timer for two minutes and draw yourself TAKING UP SPACE. In your drawing, include the WHOLE BODY. (No stick figures. Real bodies take up more space.)

Extra credit:

Write a love letter to this self-portrait. List at least three reasons you find this self-portrait delightful. Be very specific.

Extra-Extra credit:

Draw a self-portrait whenever you want. You can make up a scenario. Choose an action verb. It can be something you can't literally do in life. Or ask a friend for an action for the prompt. It's fun! It's fun to draw.

This chapter was adapted from the work of Lynda Barry.

DANCE PARTY
4

Today, you get to be the DJ.

Make a list of songs that make you feel good and happy. Whatever music delights you.

Listen to these songs regularly, on purpose. Repeat as necessary. The positive feelings you get from these songs and their messages—especially because they come from music—may start to nudge out the voice of that certain unhelpful someone. This actually works—sometimes my feel-good songs jump into my head spontaneously.

Dance whenever you feel like it.

If you want to, share your list with a friend, or hum or sing the songs whenever you require an energy shift or some sunshine.

You'll have your own songs. Here are some of mine: Anne Harris, "Lullaby"; Prince, "I Would Die 4 U" (esp. the cover by Anne Harris); Talking Heads, "This Must Be The Place"; Staples Singers, "I'll Take You There"; Curtis Mayfield, "Move On Up"; Singing Sweet, "When I See You Smile"; Waco Brothers, "Plenty Tough & Union Made";

Erykah Badu, "Back In The Day"; Pharrell Williams, "Happy"; Sufjan Stevens, "Chicago"; Bruno Mars, "Uptown Funk"; Style Council, "You're The Best Thing"; The Roots, "You Got Me" (esp. live with Jill Scott and Erykah Badu); Belle and Sebastian, "If She Wants Me"; Muwosi, "Who I Am"; Ini Kamoze, "Here Comes The Hotstepper"; Pentatonix, "Cheerleader"; Snoop Dogg, "Beautiful" . . .

Extra credit:
Sing even louder.

DRAW THE INNER CRITIC   5

On an index card or blank piece of paper, draw a frame.

Inside the frame, draw an open or a closed shape. (Either is perfect.) An open shape has ends that *don't connect*—a squiggle, doodle, flourish, etc. A closed shape has ends that *connect*—a circle, triangle, amoeba, etc. This activity should take about three seconds.

Turn your page/shape sideways, or upside down.

Set a timer for two minutes.

Start with the shape you made, and draw your inner critic as a character. No need to overthink, or think at all.

Keep the pen moving on the paper until the time is up. You can add textures, patterns, shading, scales, feathers, fangs, pinstripes, polka dots, overcoats, etc.

When the time is up, give your inner critic a name. Write the name on the page.

If the inner critic is taunting you, or maybe even if not: turn the drawing face down so they can't see you.

This chapter was adapted from the work of Lynda Barry.

Or throw it in the trash, or dance on the paper, bury it, use it to line your cat box, etc. You are also welcome to display this drawing with pride.

Now that the inner critic has moved from a voice in your thoughts to a visible character on paper, take a moment to notice any sensations or emotions that arise. Write down what you notice.

Extra credit:
Do a power pose for up to two minutes whenever you think of it, maybe every day.

DEAR INNER CRITIC (A LETTER) 6

Using the guidelines for freewriting, write a letter to your inner critic.

Set a timer for five minutes. Write the words *Dear Inner Critic*, and keep writing until the time is up.

Young people sometimes ask, "Can I use bad words?" (Yes, you can use bad words.)

If it feels okay, and you have a few more minutes, skim your letter and choose a line that stands out. Then write a P.S. that starts with that line or thought. Or you can write "And another thing," and unroll any other thing/s you need to say. This is one way to make your own prompt from what's already on the page. (You can use this trick for any sort of writing, actually.)

When you're finished, sign your letter.

Do whatever you want with the letter. Keep, burn, laminate, recycle, or use it to wrap a fish. If you can find their address and this sounds interesting: put the letter in an envelope, add a stamp, and mail it to your inner critic.

Extra credit:

Check in with yourself. Move, stretch, shake it off. Do you need some self-care? Do that thing.

Dear Inner Critic,
You know I can draw. You've seen me do it. You know I can. So why do you hound me? I know. I know why. By now, I know it's because you're scared. Scared I'll look dumb. But who cares if I look dumb? I mean, it's not like those dreams I used to have (didn't we all?) where I went to school and suddenly realized I was still in my pajamas. That embodied vulnerability. This is not like that. Also — Kids wear pajamas to school on purpose now. Evidently, we're evolving. So lay off.
Love,
⭐ Rebecca

WRITE
A DIALOGUE

7

Set a timer for five minutes.
   Write a dialogue between you and the inner critic.
   The only rule is that you get to have the first line.
   And you get to have the last line.

Extra credit:
Set a timer for one minute and freewrite what you *didn't* say to the inner critic.

MAKE A SCENE 8

Write a scene that involves you and your inner critic.

Set a timer and freewrite for five minutes.

It might be a physical fight scene. Or some other confrontation. Or a dance scene! Or any situation that involves action—or possibly inaction. Any situation that puts the two of you together in a certain place and time.

Make the scene as detailed as possible. Where are you? Is there anyone else around? Is there music? Can you smell anything in particular? Describe whatever you notice about the scene. How does the fight or dance or whatever scene escalate? What happens? See where it goes. How does it end? *Does* it end?

If it feels okay to do so, look back at your scene and underline phrases or words or sentences or images that seem in some way alive, or like they need to be underlined.

Extra credit:
Are you wearing your shoulders as earrings?[†] If so, let them drop. Repeat as necessary, not just today.

[†] My mother first heard this phrase from Camille Marie Willis, who heard it from her massage therapist.

DRAW A COMIC

9

Today, you get to draw a comic strip! It's okay if you have no idea how. You don't have to set a timer, but you can if it helps.

With words or pictures or both, sketch an idea for a simple scene. Imagine (and describe/show) a beginning, middle, and end.

You might base the scene on something you discovered from a previous activity (for example a line from the letter, or the **Make A Scene** activity).

You might imagine that you and your inner critic have a job to do and must cooperate. Something physical or embodied. Moving furniture. Cleaning the kitchen. In a car, figuring out directions for a road trip. Cleaning debris from a demolished building. Giving swimming lessons. (You get the idea.)

No need to overthink any of this.

Using index cards or a piece of paper, draw three empty frames in a horizontal row. Draw your simple scene (no stick figures).

Extra credit:

Make a list of fun or funny activities you could do with the inner critic. Let them be ridiculous or soothing or whatever. Maybe even draw a picture of the fun activity.

NOTICE AND COUNTERACT 10

Pay attention to your thoughts today. Keep an index card or notebook handy. Notice when you feel or hear the voice of self-doubt. Notice when you hear the inner critic squawk. Speak or write down a rebuttal. Take notes.

Extra credit:

Now that you know what you know from what you've done so far, loop back to the opening of this book. See which practices might sustain your energy for this continuing experiment. Power pose? Revisit the greeters list from **Assemble Your Greeters**? More foil stars? Make a plan to do some simple, easy self-care at least three days this week.

BOUNDARIES AND BUSY WORK

II

"Writing[†] is a head game. The first person who has to believe you're a writer is you."

—Connie Schultz, Antioch Writers' Workshop Keynote, 2018

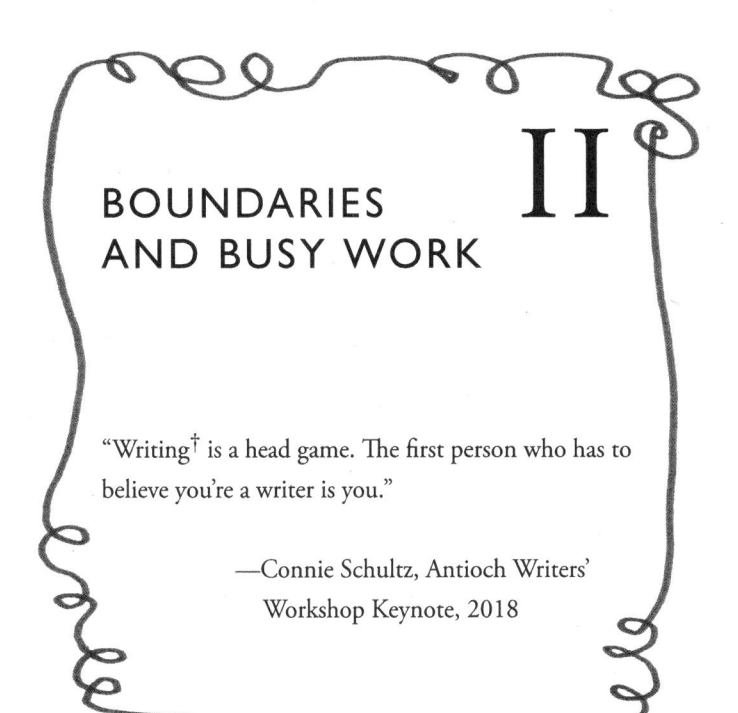

[†] Swap the word 'writing' with anything about which you are passionate—it's still applicable. Even simply being human.

NONVIOLENCE? REALLY?

11

Though the inner critic might not always evoke nonviolence from you, today, let's give it a try.

Write a letter to your inner critic. They did something you are not happy about.

Use this outline to write four sentences:
1. Fact: State the fact of what they did.
2. Feeling: State how you feel about what they did.
3. Need: State what you need from them.
4. Request: State what you request from them.

You can elaborate in the letter, or leave it at these four statements. If it feels okay, read the statements aloud. If you want, you can read them aloud to the inner critic, or convey the message in some other way.

This chapter was adapted from Nonviolent Communication, a communication framework based on principles of nonviolence.

> Dear Inner Critic,
> You said I couldn't do anything right. I felt really stupid and bad when you said that. I need to feel strong and confident!
> From now on, please refrain from saying that I can't do anything right.
> Love,
> Rebecca

Extra credit:

Take a one-minute (or longer) dance break.

GET A JOB 12

Write for five minutes.

Write a job description for your inner critic. List specific responsibilities, whatever you want to include, and don't forget *other duties as assigned.* Maybe you want the inner critic to provide earnest support to you, or to stay away. You can give them so much work they have no time for sleep. You can assign them household tasks: *do the laundry, wash the dishes, clean the litter box.*

You get to create this job. It doesn't have to be a real world type job, but it can be. It can also be an unwieldy pile of different jobs. The inner critic may leave you alone when overextended, or otherwise occupied. (They don't call it occupation for nothing.) Describe the job in as much detail as possible.

Extra credit:
Invite the inner critic to apply for the job. Imagine this freaky entity is the most qualified candidate. Hire them, or don't. Even if they are the most qualified: *You do not have*

to hire them. You could call them in for several interviews and then choose not to hire them. You don't need a reason. This is your imagination! If you do hire them, reiterate the terms of employment. Remind them you are the boss. You can tell them to stay home whenever you want to. You will write the performance reviews, and approve or deny raises, and add new duties as you see fit.

PERFECT COMEBACKS — 13

On the left margin of a blank page, write the numbers 1-10.

Then write a list of ten comebacks you can use to deflect, debunk, or annihilate the inner critic's unhelpful chatter.

These comebacks could be sentences, phrases, or words. Because they are made of a magical, neutralizing substance, your comebacks are 100% guaranteed to work. You have the power to make effective remedies.

You can use bad words. You can be ultra-polite. You can use comebacks in any language. You can use a physical gesture, or create a DELETE button, or whatever works.

Pick your favorite/s from the list (maybe all of them), and write them on a piece of paper or index card. Decorate the list with foil stars or any visuals that will enhance their effectiveness. Practice any gestures until they feel natural. Mix and match! Refer to the list/gesture/s as needed. Memorize what you can. Carry the list with you as a reminder.

Notice how it feels to have such potent options. With use, you might fine-tune the formulas to make them even stronger. See if anything shifts when you use your comebacks.

Extra credit:

Write three things in your life for which you feel gratitude. Large, or small, or in between. Write a bit about why you are grateful for these things. Why gratitude? Because even if you feel it for just one moment, that drop of gratitude can be an antidote for despair. (I've tried it. It works!)

DESIGNATE SPACE

14

Imagine a real or fictional place where you would love to live. Ideally, the space will include defined borders/edges/walls of some sort—a tent is fine, but probably not a wide-open field.

Write for five minutes. Describe the space. If possible, engage each of the senses (sight, sound, touch, taste, smell). Describe the colors, décor, contents, and anything else you notice about this dwelling and setting.

Then write a note to the inner critic. Or draw a map. Tell the inner critic where they are and are not welcome. Which parts of the space (if any) are they allowed to enter? And under what circumstances? Must they remove their shoes (if they wear shoes)? Do they have to stay in the yard, or on the back porch? Or a hundred miles away? Or somewhere else? Be as specific as possible.

And, if it feels helpful: think about your actual dwelling. Designate a nook, a room, or corner where the inner critic is NEVER allowed to be. Not ever. It can be a chair. Some place in your yard, if you have a yard. Up in a tree. The fire escape. Some spot that is just for you. If it's not simple to claim this space at home, choose a café, or the library, or some other space where you like to go. From now on, you can go there to fully escape the inner critic. You can go there in real life and/or in your imagination.

On an index card, write the name of the place, or draw the place or something that reminds you of the place. Or use a photo of the place. Then decorate the borders with magical boundary-fortification doodles, colors, stars—you know what you need to make it work.

Extra credit:

Sit quietly for a moment. What does it feel like to set boundaries with your inner critic? Notice any sensations in your body. Do you feel tightness, expansion, warmth, coolness, tension, non-tension, tingling? Numbness? Anything else? There is no need to judge or change the sensations. Simply notice what your body is feeling. Take a deep breath and let it out. Let gravity hold you. Gravity is holding you. Feel the sense of being held. After you're finished taking a moment, write what you notice.

TO DO TODAY   15

This activity can be especially helpful in the morning, on a day when you need the inner critic to leave you alone. When you have extra challenge at work or home, or a conversation you are dreading, etc. But it's also useful anytime.

If you do this at the end of the day, you can assign the TO DO list for the next day. Sometimes I reassure the inner critic that I will take care of myself and don't need their help. I excuse them for the day so they can do something else, away from me. Redirection. Redirection sometimes works with toddlers, too, at least for a moment.

Write a list of five real or imagined tasks for your inner critic to do. Circle one, and describe the task—tell them what to do, in detail.

> Dear Inner Critic,
> You see those cans and bottles of hazardous waste in the shed? Take them to the dump today. Don't spill anything. Thank the people who work at the dump. And make me a sandwich. (You'll need to make some bread first.)
> Love,
> Rebecca

Extra credit:

Write a directive for any or all of the other tasks on your list. Use this tactic whenever you need to excuse the inner critic for the day.

FUTURE FRIEND   16

If you're feeling friendless, write a letter to the future friend who's out there somewhere. The future friend is someone you can talk to about anything. Tell the friend how you're feeling today. Ask them how they're feeling.

Plan your eventual meet-up, and write it into a brief scene or invitation. Include and describe as many of the senses as possible.

Extra credit:
Write a thank you note to the friend. Express gratitude for whatever happened that time when you met up.

VERY CONTRARY

17

Today's invitation is to do something deliberately disobedient.

Make a list of ten or more things that the inner critic has discouraged you from doing or held you back from doing or said you should absolutely never, ever do.

Circle one thing on the list.

Spend five minutes writing about that thing. You might start with a phrase like "the inner critic told me never to . . . " fill in the blank, then keep going. Or write the thing you circled, and freewrite from there. If it's something imaginary that you cannot *literally* do but could *want* to do, write a scene or story where you are doing that thing. Include as much sensory detail as possible.

If the thing you circled is something that you *can* actually do, make a plan to do it. Map out your plan, schedule a date and time, and do it.

Extra credit:
Do that thing *today*.

IMAGINE A CHEERLEADER   18

Today, unexpectedly and despite everything... your inner critic woke up in a joyful mood and decided to become your fully-committed cheerleader.

What will they say and do?

First, draw a two-minute picture of the inner critic as your cheerleader. Let their exuberance and rah-rah really show in some big ways. Hint: Maybe they look like a classic cheerleader, but maybe they don't. Cheerleaders can take a variety of forms.

Then, write all the beautiful, positive, supportive things they will say and do. Be as specific as possible. This writing can be a list or paragraph/s. Just capture it all, every drop of supportive goodness from this perhaps unusual (and maybe unexpected) source.

Maybe you want to use some foil stars today.

Extra credit:

Write for a couple of minutes about whether you have noticed any softening feelings (gratitude? love?) for the inner critic. If you haven't noticed any softening, write about that.

PERFORMANCE REVIEW   19

The inner critic has been hard at work for a long time. Today, you get to write a performance review.

Describe the job and how they have been doing. Include any relevant details. List at least three areas that need improvement and how you want them to change. If—and only if—they have been doing a sufficient job, you might mention that. But don't let their recent cheerleading obscure memories of how they typically act.

What (if any) professional development is available to them? Hint: It might not actually be helpful. The professional development seminar might very boring. Busy work. That's fine!

What consequences do they face if they don't meet your expectations? Be specific and include plenty of details.

Extra credit:
Find a fun new way to hydrate or otherwise fortify yourself today. Add lemon or cucumber or ginger to your water, something that tastes really good. Enjoy!

AN UNEXPECTED GIFT

20

There's an unexpected package outside your front door, addressed to you. You open the package. Inside you find a surprisingly generous and thoughtful apology gift from your inner critic.

Is there a card? Does the card say what they are apologizing for? How is the gift wrapped? What's in the package? Describe it fully.

Then decide whether—and how—to respond to the gift.

Write your response (or non-response) to the inner critic.

Extra credit:

Give *yourself* a gift today—something even more special than a foil star. Bonus points if it's handmade. Bonus points if it doesn't cost any money. (Turns out you can get very creative with a budget of $0.)

III

TOWARD (SELF-)COMPASSION

"The world doesn't need more silenced mothers."

—Ariel Gore, Zoom meeting, Mavens of Mythmaking, 2023

SOUNDS OF DISTRESS 21

You are in the kitchen washing dishes and you hear someone crying in another room. They sound very distressed. You go look, and discover it's your inner critic.

Where are they, and what are they doing? Why are they distressed? How do you respond?

Write the scene. Include some mention of music.

Extra credit:

Look back at your response to the **Designate Space** activity. Consider whether you want to revise the list of spaces where your inner critic is or is not allowed and under which conditions. Jot down any thoughts about this, even if you are not changing anything—which is worth noting, too.

WHO CARES WHAT THEY NEED? 22

You care.

Why? Because considering unmet need/s might help you understand why the inner critic sometimes acts like such a gnat.

For five minutes, freewrite. Speculate about what the inner critic needs. If it helps, start with a list.

Why do you think they must constantly tear you down?

What are they lacking?

Write any details or messages that come up.

Extra credit:

Take a dance break. Play a song from your **Dance Party** list, or something else that makes you feel good.

HOW YOU PROVED (OR WILL PROVE) THEM WRONG

23

Fill in the blanks: "They always said I would have to/couldn't/shouldn't/wouldn't (_____) but I (_____) anyway."

This can be something you have already achieved. Or it can be a future action or plan. Change the verb tenses as needed. After you fill in the blanks, spend five minutes freewriting about how you proved them wrong, or how you will.

Extra credit:
Identify the source of the original message—who or what is "they"? Did the inner critic absorb and plant the message as if it was fact? Was the message supported by aspects of the larger culture/s?

If it feels okay, jot down some ideas about how you might uproot that message. Imagine how freeing it would be to neutralize and release that trash. That non-fact. Write a scene or whatever seems useful.

CHOOSE YOUR OWN ADVENTURE

24

If it feels okay, take a few minutes to glance back at what you've done thus far. You don't have to read closely, just skim what came from previous activities. Aim for a detached curiosity. Relax your eyes, if it helps. Or let your hands hover above the pages in your notebook or index cards until something seems to say, *Choose me!*

There's something waiting there. Notice what has a pulse, what grabs your attention—maybe a phrase, an activity you loved or hated or skipped, a drawing. Anything that shimmers or quivers.

Maybe it's an activity that wants a do-over. Maybe it's a phrase or nugget of discovery that haunts you. Relax your body.

Start with that activity, phrase, or nugget and spend five or more minutes freewriting about it.

Extra credit:
Take an extra big drink of water. (Take another drink until you feel fully quenched. Ahhh, that's better.)

DEAR RISK MANAGER 25

A risk manager is in charge of safety and security. A risk manager aims to detect and avoid the possibility of harm, from major devastation to minor bumps and bruises.

Today, write a letter to the inner critic in their capacity as risk manager. Hint: in the context of self-doubt and the inner critic, risk management often comes from fear.

Start your letter with the words *Dear Risk Manager* . . .

In your letter, ask what's at risk. What are they trying to protect you from? What are they afraid of? If you're not sure, you can guess. Give yourself full permission to speculate on the page. Write for five minutes.

Extra credit:

Write a list of three to ten theoretical situations in which the inner critic's protection might be helpful or even welcome. The situations can be wildly fictional. *If a piano was about to fall on my head, and my inner critic shoved me out of the way, I'd be grateful.* And maybe there is no situation where you would want their help. If that's the case, write a list of anything else you *don't* want them to do. More boundaries. That's fine! As Robert Frost wrote, "Good fences make good neighbors."

WHAT ARE THEY TRYING TO TELL YOU?

26

Refer to the activity called **Assemble Your Greeters**. Assemble (or re-assemble) your greeters.

Close or relax your eyes, and take a moment to imagine the scene and the greeters in detail. Stay with imagining until you feel the greeters are solid and ready to support you.

When your greeters are solid, imagine the inner critic standing in front of you—far enough away that you have a comfortable boundary. Ask the inner critic if there's anything they need to say to you. In some way, let the inner critic know they are safe, and you will listen.

Allow time for the inner critic to answer. Maybe they won't say anything for a while. All you have to do for now is listen.

When you feel ready, allow a resolution to this

This chapter was adapted from the work of Richard Schwartz, Internal Family Systems.

interaction. Maybe it's simple: you listened and heard their message. Maybe there's something you want to say to them. If so, say it.

Spend a few minutes writing any messages, feelings, or whatever you notice. No need to judge or figure anything out. You're just taking notes.

Extra credit:
Did what came up surprise you? If so, write about that. Then spend at least a few minutes outside, or open a window. Get some fresh air.

A DIFFERENT GIFT 27

Now it's your turn to do some gift giving.

If you could give your inner critic a gift today, what would it be? And why? There are no parameters. The gift does not have to be nice or pleasant, but it can be. If you're having trouble thinking of something appropriate, write a list of ten (even random) options, and choose whatever seems to fit.

Describe the gift: hand-me-down, handmade, store-bought, or found at the side of the road? How is it wrapped? Is there a card? What do you write on the card?

Describe the moment of giving the gift. How does the inner critic react?

Write the scene. Include at least five lines of dialogue.

Extra credit:
Did anything that came up in this one surprise you? Write for a couple of minutes about what and why.

THE SANDBOX   28

Imagine you and your inner critic are both children. You are in a sandbox together. Notice what you notice about both of you. How are you dressed? What are you doing in the sandbox? Are there toys? Any other kids around? Adults? What's the weather like?

Describe the situation in detail, including the setting. Location, sights, sounds, smells, textures. You can draw, or write, or both.

What happens?

Extra credit:
Get some actual fresh air, or try a type of food or beverage that you've never had (or all of the above).

DEAR YOU   29

Today, the first part is to do something to make yourself feel good. Power pose, or dance party, anyone? Or take a walk. Or do something of your own devising that cheers you up (if you're grumpy) or helps sustain your already-good mood.

Then, imagine you are playing the role of the inner critic.

Sit and breathe for a moment with this imagining.

Set a timer for five to seven minutes.

Write a letter FROM the inner critic TO you. Write "*Dear* (your name)." Based on what you know about your inner critic, make up what you think they would say in a letter to you. You don't have to hold back. You can be lavish, extreme, unrestrained. The letter can be wild, needy, ridiculous, loving, or "badly written," whatever that means. Don't overthink it.

But somewhere in the letter, include a reference to a book from your childhood. If you need a place to start, start there.

Extra credit:
Resume being yourself. Write a response letter to the inner critic, from the real you. Then shake it off, literally. Shake your body. Remind yourself that this can be really hard work, and you are doing it anyway!

EMPTY NEST

30

Imagine your inner critic is gone, gone, gone. Found another place to hang out. Vanished. Poof! Gone.

Using the guidelines for drawing, draw a picture of who you are now, with your inner critic gone.

Take a few minutes to color it in. Write words of inspiration in the drawing if you want to.

Place the drawing where you can see it.

Remember who you are.

Extra credit:
Write a poem about who you are now.

P.S. It doesn't matter if you don't know how to write a poem. The poem doesn't have to be good, whatever that means. The poem just has to exist.

WHAT COMES NEXT?

"Everyone gets an A for napping."

> —Lynda Barry, "Writing the Unthinkable,"
> Omega Institute, 2016

Dear You,

You did it! You spent 30 days doing creative things because you wanted to. You tried new things. Silly things, sometimes. Maybe some days you didn't feel like it, but did things anyway. Maybe you listened to music, and maybe you danced. You drank water. And wrote words and drew pictures where previously, there was nothing. Maybe you drew a person who was not made of sticks. Maybe you took care of yourself on purpose. Even if your motivation was to earn extra credit or foil stars—you did it. Even if you skipped a day or activity here and there, you made it to *now*, to read these words—you did it!

Now, how will you celebrate? My advice: do

something, maybe something tangible, like make a drawing or write yourself a letter, that honors the fact that your creative spirit is this much closer to liberation. Notice how this new state of being feels. Keep in touch with what you've discovered.

Always, you can refer back to any activities you found helpful. And dream up your own, too.

Thank you for playing!
> Love,
> Rebecca

P.S. The experience of feeling self-doubt is probably not over. Maybe it will never be over. But I hope that now you can see it as a passing cloud rather than a built-in condition of your existence. You have lots of tools. You have everything you need. You can sustain ongoing renegotiations with the inner critic. Maybe you feel a subtle (or beyond subtle) shift in how self-doubt happens within you. Maybe you feel the burden is lighter.

More Activities

Using the guidelines for free writing, write a letter to your inner critic every day for 30 days, ideally first thing in the morning. Notice what shifts and what stays constant, or anything else that happens.

✳ ✳ ✳

From the products of any of these activities, take a fragment, idea, phrase, image, and freewrite. See what happens. Hint: I promise you will find that your own natural human intelligence is infinitely better than artificial intelligence at generating ideas and solutions!

✳ ✳ ✳

Look back at what you've done. Notice trends and themes. Write for a few minutes, reflecting on what you found and what you might want to do with the information. If it fits, make a plan to do whatever things (small, medium, large, or extra-large) will lead you away from suffering and toward joy.

✳ ✳ ✳

Do an activity from this book with someone you trust. Make a plan about how (or if) to talk about the activity after you finish. Do you want to share, or pass? If you share, take turns listening to each other without comment. You can simply thank each other. Or if you want to comment, ask permission first. Consent is beautiful. Let it be confidential. Be real and cheer each other on. Connect in a way that feels mutual and supportive and safe.

✵ ✵ ✵

If you notice that your inner critic resembles a person in your life (past or present), you might get curious, slow down, and investigate further—if it feels safe. Refer to the greeters, and do self-care as needed. If your inner critic is a composite of toxic self-loathing from various sources, you could play with making it into an extreme character. Exaggerate its features. Give it awful breath. Go big! Write and draw.

✵ ✵ ✵

Do even more self-care, whenever you can or want to. You don't need a reason and you don't have to tell anyone.

✵ ✵ ✵

Look up the people mentioned in the **Backstory and Acknowledgements** and **Resources** sections. Request their books from the library, or buy them if you can. For products, shop at the source, and support independent bookstores whenever possible. In this way, you support the people who supported this book.

✷ ✷ ✷

Plan how to continue your self-doubt renegotiation. How will you interact with the inner critic, now that you have met and conversed? How will you keep the communication going? Return to self-care. And remember that self-care can be very simple, can be little moments. Time outside, fresh air, water, breath. A cup of tea. Curiosity about something you see. An even closer look at something you see. Dance. Write down your plan and keep it handy.

BACKSTORY AND ACKNOWLEDGEMENTS

This book evolved from a mighty lineage. I am grateful to the openhearted humans who helped—whether they knew they were helping or not.

As mentioned earlier, in the 1990s, I participated in Py Bateman's feminist self-defense class, Alternatives to Fear. Back then, another self-defense class—Model Mugging—had a man in a padded suit jump out to grab you (to simulate the element of surprise). But Alternatives to Fear came from a more empowering framework—what we might now call *trauma-informed*. This was where I first learned how to set boundaries within a context of safety and healing.

In 2014, at the Antioch Writers' Workshop, Gayle Brandeis said, "The faster I write, the more I'm able to outrun my self-doubt." This single sentence reframed my thoughts about self-doubt—it became possible to outrun, or at least I decided to try. (Thanks, Gayle!) Bonni Goldberg, in her book *Room to Write*, includes a prompt called "Critical Mass": turn the inner voice of self-doubt into a character, and describe it. That prompt had a profound impact on my students (and me) because it uses the familiar process of creating a character. Lynda Barry employed a method from a 16th century Japanese Zen monk to paint what haunts you, which resulted in her book *One! Hundred! Demons!* In 2016, I took a workshop with Lynda Barry called "Writing The Unthinkable." She teaches non-judgmental ways to draw and write—and the lack of judgment amplified the oxygen in the room. To discover that a workshop could be so rejuvenating and didn't have to include the usual self-doubt, loathing, and anxiety revolutionized my creative life and my focus as a teacher and mentor. (Lynda Barry changed my life.)

Melissa Benton Barker, Amy Rebekah Chavez and I collaborated on workshops to embody creative self-expression. We used yoga, writing, and somatic practices to create opportunity for healing. Climbing Poetree (especially the poem "Being Human") provided inspiration, starting with the question, *I wonder.* Brené Brown demystified vulnerability and the gremlins of shame. Amy Cuddy's power poses helped me become more confident. Denise Jacobs' book, *Banish Your Inner Critic*, overflows with practical advice for boosting creative power. Laraine Herring's leadership (in teaching, editing, and what she writes) offers inspiration for the long haul, and deep and abiding nuances of self-compassion to inform the writing process. Resmaa Menakem's book *My Grandmother's Hands* illuminates generational trauma and how the body holds pain. And how, with practice, support, and intention, we can release our pain. Anne Eberhardt introduced me to Internal Family Systems—the parts of the self, specifically the inner critic.

* * *

All these ingredients went into the cooking-pot.

* * *

At some point, an idea surfaced: *What if I write a letter to my inner critic every day for thirty days?* I did it. During that month, I began to understand the machinery of my self-doubt. Inside me, things began to shift toward creative liberation.

There's power and simplicity in writing a letter. A letter—as a form of writing—is very accessible. And even when the writing is digressive or muddled, a letter can become an arrow, headed straight toward what really matters.

Inspired by these sources and experiments, I developed a workshop called *Dear Inner Critic*, which I've presented at schools, universities, libraries, and other community spaces.

I wrote this book by expanding material from that workshop and translating it to the page.

Thanks to all who experimented with me. Students, peers, friends, family, trusted therapists, and comrades helped me sustain and refine these offerings . . . and helped me survive and thrive as a person in the world.

✯ ✯ ✯

To all Rabbit's Friends-and-Relations: love, love, love.

Without the light-seeing-and-making force of nature known as Ariel Gore, this chapbook (and a million other beautiful things) would not exist. Huge gratitude to Ariel; Zena Sharman; Patricia Harrelson; Sue Moshofsky; China Martens; Jen Antill; Jessica Beard; Christa Orth; the Mavens of Mythmaking; and the Chapbook Challenge creators for unparalleled connection and magic. *I cannot imagine a more ideal editorial board of wayward geniuses being geniuses together.*

Gratitude to the Maneri family, esp. the three sisters, my original sirens of creativity, for everything they made—especially the humans—and (almost) everyone they married; to Bev Price, Bill Mullins, and Margaret Landes at the Antioch School; to middle school language arts teacher Cindy Mapes, who opened those magical composition book doors; to Virginia Hamilton, Arnold Adoff, and Don Wallis for early and sustained encouragement. To my father, David Kuder, for publishing my first chapbook (*The Hole In The Shirt*, Earth Free School Press, 1974) . . .

Always, always, gratitude to many writing groups over many years, especially *yes yes yes* the beloved Girdles, for infinite stretch from one century into the next . . . Chris Benda; Lisa Horowitz Brooks; Elaine Gale; Candace Kearns Read; Julia Kress; Victoria Morsell Hemingson; Vanja Thompson; and Kristin Walrod . . .

For support of body and soul, ideas, inspiration, consultation, manuscript-reading, flying lessons and other ineffables, love and gratitude to Amy Chavez; Melissa Benton Barker; Patrick Lacey; Chris Benda; Anne Harris; Kristen Speagle; Linda Pandey; Jeni Felker; Chris Tebbetts; Felicia Chappelle; Arden Miller; Sean Egan; Miles Cuddy; The Houses of Korpieski-Hinson-Korson, Hoff-Miyazaki, and Sage-Frabotta; Vanessa Hale; Deborah Leigh Clark; Anne Eberhardt; Liz Griffin; Tia Acheson; Kelli Zaytoun; Sally Lamping; Diane Baumer; Dee Krieg; Maxine Skuba; Laurie Dreamspinner; Marybeth Wolf; Nicole Rosaria Manieri; Kirsten Bean; Ashley Lackovich-Van Gorp; the red tent sisterhood; Jahzerah Brooks; Emma Margraf; Audra King; Rachel Fulkerson; Paula Hurwitz; Jaimie Wilke; Mary Hallinan; Laurel Finch; Kayla Graham and Maya Trujillo of GravityWorks Circus; Jon Langford; Eloise Klein Healy; Jim Krusoe; Tara Ison; Rod Val Moore and everyone at What Books Press; Andromeda Romano-Lax;

Virginia Watts; Divyam Chaya Bernstein, Barbi Beckett, and Dana Mezzina; Nick Flynn; Dina Peone; Mark Alexander (*thanks for the holiday!*); and especially my mother, Margaret Alexander . . .

Thanks to independent booksellers, including Kate Mooneyham and Gail Lichtenfels.

The Emporium! Scientifically Proven to be the Best Place in the World. Thanks to Kurt Miyazaki and all who sustain that space.

For help and support, here and everywhere: Robert Freeman Wexler and Merida Serena Kuder-Wexler, I love you. Thank you for making this book (and life) with me.

Gratitude to all (named and unnamed) who informed and inspired the item you hold in your hands.

And gratitude to you, reader, for allowing me to share these practices with you, now.

RESOURCES

Understanding and Healing Trauma and Other Helpful Items

The offerings of these healers have helped support my body, spirit, and understanding of how we can heal ourselves and others.

Amy Rebekah Chavez: ReStoryative Somatics—"a therapeutic model of trauma healing with a focus on nervous system regulation, emotional resilience, physical, and relational healing." www.lovesomatics.org

Somatic Experiencing (with database of providers): www.traumahealing.org

Resmaa Menakem, *My Grandmother's Hands*

Emmett E. Miller, "Releasing Shame, Embracing Self-Worth" (guided meditation)

Bessel van der Kolk, *The Body Keeps The Score*

Andrew Weil, 4-7-8 breath video: tinyurl.com/27aerr9p

Writers, Music, and Other Sources of Inspiration

These creative humans have provided inspiration in life and in the work with my inner critic. I hope you will enjoy what they have to offer, too.

Lynda Barry
Books: *One! Hundred! Demons!* and *Syllabus*, etc.
Videos: "Accessing the Imaginary" tinyurl.com/msvajbac; "The answer is in the picture" tinyurl.com/4xm273h7 (Watch the mom respond about the bacon!) Instagram: tinyurl.com/urcjyw7j
Gayle Brandeis: www.gaylebrandeis.com
Brené Brown: tinyurl.com/bdf2576p
Amy Cuddy (power poses): tinyurl.com/yrbe5h3b
Ross Gay (delights): www.rossgay.net
Bonni Goldberg, *Room To Write* ("Critical Mass")
Ariel Gore: *The Wayward Writer,* etc. www.arielgore.com
Anne Harris: www.anneharris.com
Laraine Herring: tinyurl.com/2m6dsdxz
Denise Jacobs, *Banish Your Inner Critic*
Jon Langford: tinyurl.com/ye2ywhhw
Naima Penniman, "Being Human": tinyurl.com/5n87vbsp
Sol Rising Transformative Arts Troupe (healing circle songs): tinyurl.com/3x6ce65x
Melissa Benton Barker: www.melissabentonbarker.com/bio

Self-Care and Nourishment

Hooray for those who make and do things to heal our bodies and the planet. I am grateful to know and support these loving humans for their beautiful products, made with love and intention.

Radical Self-Love Body Butter: Small-batch, organic and sustainably sourced (and delightful). tinyurl.com/4sktrepx

CommuniTea Love: Small-batch, lovingly made tea, plus workshops and healing services. www.communitealove.org/

Pepper Forrest Spice Company: "Excellent spice for all foods and all people." tinyurl.com/5kketuc7

Literary Kitchen Publications

Ariel Gore's School for Wayward Writers at the Literary Kitchen is a marvelous place to write. The Literary Kitchen offers inspiration, classes, writing prompts, and a way to connect with other wildly creative humans.

Literary Kitchen: www.literarykitchen.net/shop

ABOUT THE AUTHOR

Rebecca Kuder's debut novel is *The Eight Mile Suspended Carnival* (What Books Press, 2021). Her stories and essays have appeared in *Los Angeles Review of Books; Hags on Fire; Bayou Magazine; Shadows and Tall Trees; Year's Best Weird Fiction; The Rumpus; Crooked Houses*; and elsewhere. She received an MFA in Creative Writing from Antioch University Los Angeles and an individual artist excellence award from the Ohio Arts Council. Rebecca teaches in college, university, K-12, and community settings. She offers workshops and coaching on the creative process and how to coexist with the inner critic. She lives in Yellow Springs, Ohio, with the writer Robert Freeman Wexler and their daughter.

www.rebeccakuder.com | Instagram: @rebeccakuder